629.892 Kenney
Cutting-edge robotics

WITHDRAWN

S0-AII-753

Property of: Mentor Public Library
8215 Mentor Ave.   09/27/2018
Mentor, OH 44060

Cutting-Edge STEM

Cutting-Edge Robotics

Karen Latchana Kenney

Lerner Publications ◆ Minneapolis

Copyright © 2019 by Lerner Publishing Group, Inc.

All rights reserved. International copyright secured. No part of this book may be reproduced, stored in a retrieval system, or transmitted in any form or by any means—electronic, mechanical, photocopying, recording, or otherwise—without the prior written permission of Lerner Publishing Group, Inc., except for the inclusion of brief quotations in an acknowledged review.

Lerner Publications Company
A division of Lerner Publishing Group, Inc.
241 First Avenue North
Minneapolis, MN 55401 USA

For reading levels and more information, look up this title at www.lernerbooks.com.

Main body text set in Adrianna Regular 14/20.
Typeface provided by Chank.

Library of Congress Cataloging-in-Publication Data

Names: Kenney, Karen Latchana, author.
Title: Cutting-edge robotics / by Karen Latchana Kenney.
Description: Minneapolis, MN : Lerner Publications, [2019] | Series: Searchlight books. Cutting-edge STEM | Includes bibliographical references and index. | Audience: Ages 8–11. | Audience: Grades 4 to 6.
Identifiers: LCCN 2017059615 (print) | LCCN 2017058727 (ebook) | ISBN 9781541525399 (eb pdf) | ISBN 9781541523449 (lb : alk. paper) | ISBN 9781541527768 (pb : alk. paper)
Subjects: LCSH: Robotics—Juvenile literature.
Classification: LCC TJ211.2 (print) | LCC TJ211.2 .K44 2019 (ebook) | DDC 629.8/92—dc23

LC record available at https://lccn.loc.gov/2017059615

Manufactured in the United States of America
1-44417-34676-3/9/2018

Contents

Chapter 1

WHAT IS ROBOTICS?

A tiny object the width of a human hair motors through a mouse's stomach acid. It uses bubbles to push itself forward. Then it delivers medicine to heal sores in the mouse's stomach. This tiny object is a robot.

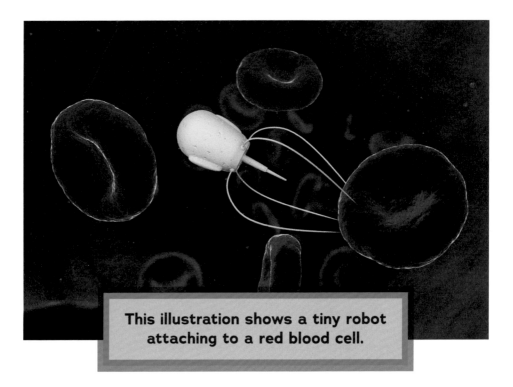

This illustration shows a tiny robot attaching to a red blood cell.

Big and Small Robots

Robots are machines that can sense and react to the world around them. Humans build and program robots. Humans control some robots. Others can perform tasks on their own. Some robots look a lot like people. Others are simply giant arms used in factories. Tiny robots called nanorobots can move in very small spaces. Many robots do work that is too dangerous or difficult for people to do.

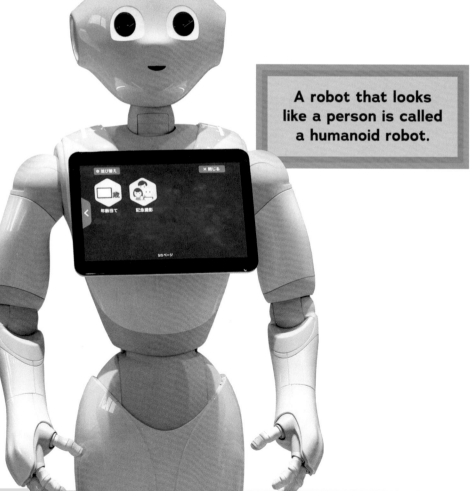

A robot that looks like a person is called a humanoid robot.

Robot Makers

People who make robots are roboticists. They design robots using computers. Roboticists create a robot's brain, the central computer that tells it what to do. Roboticists figure out how the brain will control the rest of the robot with electrical signals. Roboticists also design parts such as sensors, so the robot can see and touch things.

A roboticist may have to try several different designs before finding one that works.

Science Fact or Science Fiction?

Robots can walk just like humans.

That's false—but roboticists are working on it.

Walking on two legs may seem simple to us, but it requires a lot of coordination. Most robots on two legs lose their balance and fall over. But a robot named Cassie is almost there. This robot can walk and stay balanced on two legs, even on uneven ground.

One company is working on a robot that can walk in disaster areas filled with broken objects and rough ground.

Roboticists are good at solving problems. They think about ways robots can help people.

Robotics is about designing, making, and using robots. Roboticists are creating the machines of the future. But robots aren't just for the future—they're already being used in amazing ways.

Chapter 2

ROBOT WORKERS

At a restaurant in China, a robot greets everyone who comes inside. Robot servers deliver food to the tables, and a robot singer entertains people while they eat. Robots like these seem very smart, but are they? What you can't see are the humans that operate them. They are back in the kitchen, behind the scenes.

A robot serves guests in a robot-themed restaurant in China.

A roboticist uses a computer to control her Lego robot.

A robot server may not think, but it has a brain. The brain processes the instructions given by human operators and controls how the robot moves to complete these instructions. This brain is called the controller. The robot's controller runs on instructions written in code. People use different kinds of code to program robots. Some of the most popular coding languages are C, C++, and Python. Code written in these languages tell a robot how to move and interact with its environment.

Coding Spotlight

One of the most common coding languages used in robotics is C++. Roboticists can use this language to make robots do many things. Here is a simple code written in C++. It tells a computer to print "Hello World."

```
#include <iostream>

int main()

{

        std::cout << "Hello World!"

}
```

C++ is popular because it can organize lots of information. This language is often used for large, complicated programs.

Factory robots don't make mistakes as humans do. Robots do their tasks the same way every time.

Factory Robots

Sparks fly from a giant arm in a car factory. The arm attaches metal onto cars as they move along the assembly line. Industrial robots do the same task over and over. They are designed to work in an environment that does not change. This kind of robot is useful for only a specific task. But it can perform that task faster and better than a human could.

Robots in Space

Some robots are even in space! Canadarm2 is on the International Space Station (ISS). This robot reaches 56 feet (17 m) into space and grabs unpiloted ships delivering cargo to the astronauts living on the station.

Robonaut 2 is also on the ISS. It looks like a person. Astronauts control Canadarm2 and Robonaut 2. Astronauts enter commands into a computer on the ISS. Then the robot's controller system figures out how to perform the astronaut's commands.

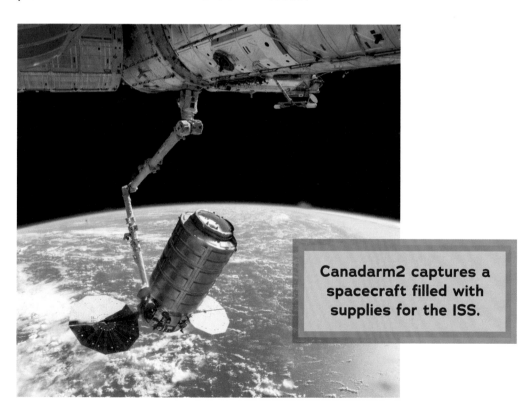

Canadarm2 captures a spacecraft filled with supplies for the ISS.

Surgical Robots

Robots can help humans with their health problems too. A surgical robot called da Vinci performs operations in many hospitals. A human surgeon controls the robot. The da Vinci system has a magnified 3D camera to help the surgeon see. Then the surgeon controls the robot to make small cuts and move in ways a human hand cannot. With this robot, surgeons can operate on heart valves, inside windpipes, and much more.

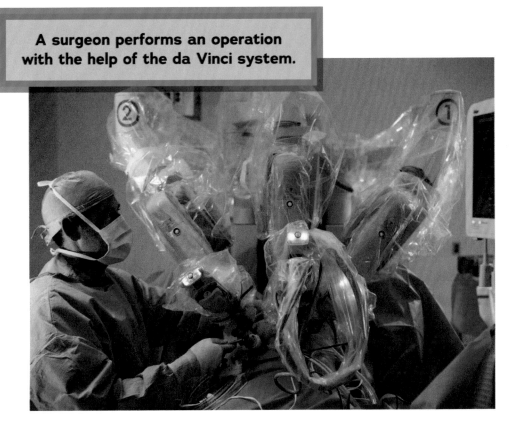

A surgeon performs an operation with the help of the da Vinci system.

Chapter 3

ROBOT EXPLORERS

Deep below the ocean surface, a robot rover creeps along the soft seafloor. The rover is the size of a riding lawn mower, and it moves on treads. As it inches along, the rover collects information about the plants and animals in the deep sea. Its sensors detect oxygen levels. They find animals such as worms in the mud. The data helps scientists understand how the water's temperature affects creatures living in the deep sea.

Researchers in Spain created this robot known as Girona 500. It can travel alone underwater to study the seafloor.

This rover is a kind of autonomous robot. It can move in an environment that changes. It doesn't need a human to constantly control how it moves or what it does. Once humans have given the robot instructions, it can explore the world on its own.

Autonomous robots work in many environments. People use them for education, entertainment, and security.

This robot can dance! It has a sensor to track motion and help it stay balanced.

Sensing the World

Robots use sensors to help them move in different environments. A camera is a sensor that shows a robot what surrounds it. A microphone allows a robot to hear. Contact sensors have switches that move when a robot bumps into something.

An infrared sensor sends out a beam of light. If the beam hits something, the light bounces back to the robot. Then the robot knows where to go and what to avoid.

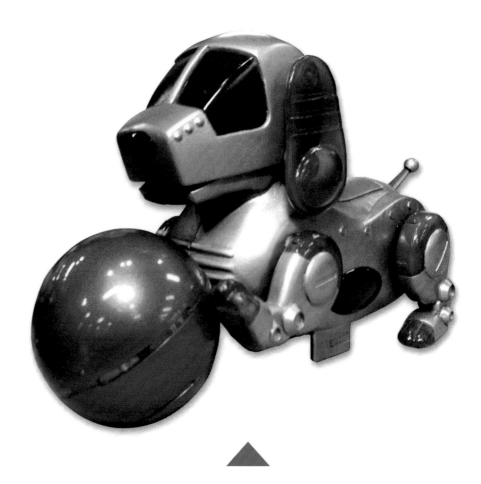

THIS ROBOTIC DOG USES AN INFRARED SENSOR TO PLAY WITH A BALL.

Moving around Mars

Two robotic explorers began investigating Mars in January 2004. These rovers, *Spirit* and *Opportunity,* drove around Mars's craters and valleys. They tested the soil and rocks and sent pictures and data back to scientists on Earth. Using their sensors and commands from Earth, the robots made their way across the unknown land. *Spirit* stopped working in 2009, but *Opportunity* has been collecting information on the planet for fourteen years. The National Aeronautics and Space Administration (NASA) is making a new robotic rover for its 2020 mission to Mars.

This illustration shows a rover on the surface of Mars.

Helpful at Home

You can even use robots in your own home or yard. One kind of robot roams the floors, sucking up all the dirt it can find. If it bumps into the couch, it knows to move in a different direction. This robotic vacuum has one job—to clean your floors.

Robot vacuum cleaners use infrared sensors and contact sensors to move around your home.

A wire around the edge of this lawn acts as an invisible fence for the robot lawn mower. That way it doesn't wander into the street or the neighbor's yard!

Another robot can climb up your windows while cleaning them. And a robotic lawn mower travels across your lawn with its rotating blades. It snips grass into shape without any human help.

These are just some of the robots people are using. Future robots may be able to do things we can only imagine.

Science Fact or Science Fiction?

You can buy a robocat if you're feeling lonely.

Yep, that's true!

Toy makers are creating furry robotic pets such as cats, dogs, and even seals. One Japanese pet called Qoobo is just a round pillow with a tail. You can pet these robots, and they react by wagging their tails, purring, and more. These pets react because they have simple sensors that tell them when they're being touched. Some nursing homes use robopets so elderly adults don't feel lonely.

This robotic seal moves its head and flippers and makes sounds like a real baby seal.

Chapter 4

ROBOTS OF THE FUTURE

Scientists are experimenting with new kinds of robots every day. Some robots work in groups. TERMES robots work together to build tall structures with stairs. One day, these kinds of robots might be able to stack sandbags on a coastline. They could protect people from a damaging hurricane that's about to hit land.

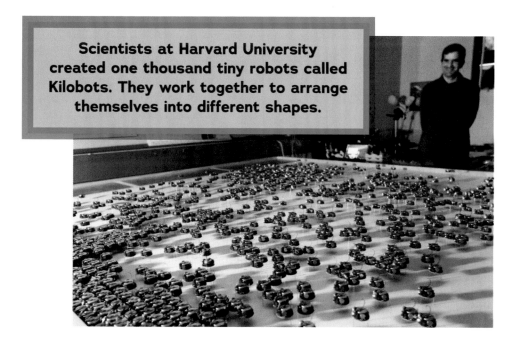

Scientists at Harvard University created one thousand tiny robots called Kilobots. They work together to arrange themselves into different shapes.

TERMES robots are swarm robots. They move and work in large numbers, the way some insects, such as termites, or schools of fish move. Scientists look to these creatures for design ideas. They try to make machines that mimic how the animals move and act.

Tiny flying robots called RoboBees might one day be used for search and rescue missions.

Robots in Action

In March 2011, an earthquake and tsunami damaged the Fukushima Daiichi nuclear plant in Japan. Nuclear fuel melted, damaging the nuclear reactors and releasing dangerous radiation. Japanese engineers created a swimming robot they called little sunfish. It is the size of a bread loaf and has propellers and cameras. The engineers hope to use the robot to find out how bad the damage is. Then scientists can figure out how to clean up the reactors.

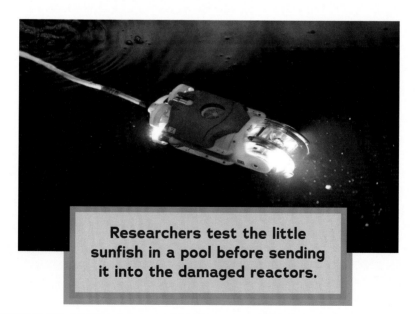

Researchers test the little sunfish in a pool before sending it into the damaged reactors.

Delivering Medicine

Nanorobots are extremely small robots. One day, doctors might inject sick people with nanorobots. Each nanorobot would carry medicine. It could swim through the blood and bring the medicine right where it needs to go.

Nanorobots filled with small amounts of medicine might one day float through a person's bloodstream.

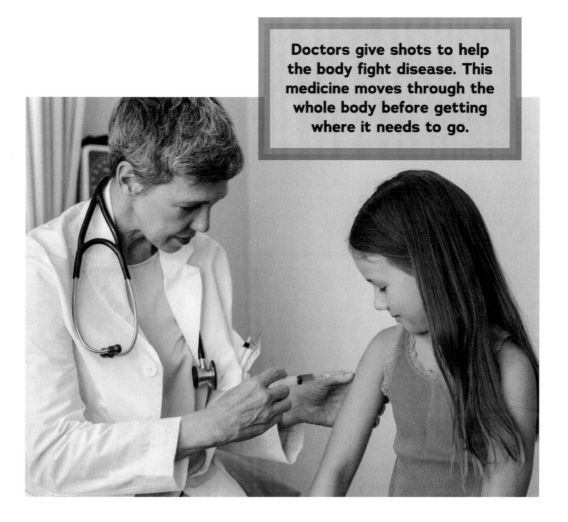

Doctors give shots to help the body fight disease. This medicine moves through the whole body before getting where it needs to go.

Putting robots in your body might sound strange. But they could keep you from having to go through a dangerous surgery. And you would only need small amounts of medicine in your body because the robot would go to exactly the right place to make you feel better.

Artificial Intelligence

Scientists are also working on artificial intelligence (AI) for robots. They hope to develop robots that can think of new ideas and learn on their own. Instead of being programmed with code, the robot could learn from experiences. Engineers are already developing AI technology. It's being tested in cars that can drive on their own. The technology company Nvidia is testing a self-driving car. Its computer learned how to drive by watching humans drive.

Self-driving cars use many sensors to stay on the road and avoid hitting people or other cars.

The robot Erica can have conversations with people about many different topics.

Someday we may live with robots that look and think just like us. One of these androids already exists in Japan. She's Erica, and she can talk, ask questions, blink, and move her head and eyes. She's an example of the future of robotics. From robonauts to nanorobots, future robots will help humans solve many kinds of problems.

Glossary

android: a robot that acts and looks like a person

autonomous: able to act on its own

code: a set of instructions that a computer can understand

controller: a robot's brain

nanorobot: a tiny robot that could fit inside a human

program: to give a computer a set of instructions

roboticist: a person who designs and builds robots

rover: a vehicle used for exploring an unknown area such as a planet

sensor: a tool that a robot uses to see, touch, and hear in its environment

tsunami: a very large wave created by an earthquake

Learn More about Robotics

Books

Higgins, Nadia. *Factory Robots*. Mankato: Amicus Ink, 2018. Find out about the machines that make and package goods in a factory.

Hustad, Douglas. *Discover Robotics*. Minneapolis: Lerner Publications, 2017. Discover the many jobs that robots do in our world.

Lindeen, Mary. *Robot Competitions*. Minneapolis: Lerner Publications, 2018. What kinds of robots do everyday people create? And which are the best? Find out in this book, along with the ways their robots compete.

Websites

NASA SpacePlace: The Mars Rovers
https://spaceplace.nasa.gov/mars-rovers/en/
Check out this site for information on the two rovers on Mars and the one planned for the 2020 mission.

NASA: What Is Robonaut?
https://www.nasa.gov/audience/forstudents/k-4/stories/nasa-knows/what-is-robonaut-k4.html
Learn about Robonaut and how it is used on the International Space Station.

STEMWorks: Robotics
http://stem-works.com/subjects/1-robotics
This site has information about robotics and other exciting STEM topics.

Index

Photo Acknowledgments

The images in this book are used with the permission of: SCIEPRO/Science Photo Library/ Getty Images, p. 4; pio3/Shutterstock.com, p. 5; science photo/Shutterstock.com, p. 6; YOSHIKAZU TSUNO/AFP/Getty Images, pp. 7, 17, 18; Gorodenkoff/Shutterstock.com, p. 8; STR/AFP/Getty Images, p. 9; Oli Scarff/Getty Images, p. 10; nd3000/Shutterstock.com, p. 11; Praphan Jampala/Shutterstock.com, p. 12; NASA/JPL, p. 13; Dana Neely/Stone/Getty Images, p. 14; BORIS HORVAT/AFP/Getty Images, p. 15; Belish/Shutterstock.com, p. 16; NASA/JPL/ Cornell University/Maas Digital, p. 19; Quality Stock Arts/Shutterstock.com, p. 20; Maya Kruchankova/Shutterstock.com, p. 21; frantic00/Shutterstock.com, p. 22; Wendy Maeda/The Boston Globe/Getty Images, p. 23; Thierry Falise/LightRocket/Getty Images, p. 24; TORU YAMANAKA/AFP/Getty Images, p. 25; KTSDESIGN/SCIENCE PHOTO LIBRARY/Getty Images, p. 26; Rido/Shutterstock.com, p. 27; Kim Kulish/Corbis/Getty Images, p. 28; Nicolas Datiche/ SIPA/Newscom, p. 29.

Front cover: Bill Stafford/NASA/JSC/Handout/Corbis/Getty Images.